THE CIVIL WAR

SHERMAN'S MARCH TO THE SEA

by Tom Streissguth

FOCUS
READERS.

VOYAGER

www.focusreaders.com

Focus Readers is distributed by North Star Editions:
sales@northstareditions.com | 888-417-0195

Produced for Focus Readers by Red Line Editorial.

Content Consultant: Dr. Gideon Mailer, Associate Professor of History, University of Minnesota Duluth

Photographs ©: Library of Congress/AP Images, cover, 1; George N. Barnard/Civil War Photographs, 1861–1865/Library of Congress, 4–5, 22–23; George N. Barnard/Buyenlarge/Archive Photos/Getty Images, 7; Everett Historical/Shutterstock Images, 8–9, 44; George N. Barnard/AP Images, 11; Civil War Photographs, 1861–1865/Library of Congress, 12, 14–15, 19, 29, 30–31; Red Line Editorial, 16, 38; Dorothea Lange/Farm Security Administration - Office of War Information Photograph Collection/ Library of Congress, 21; L. D. Andrew/Historic American Buildings Survey/Library of Congress, 25; Library of Congress, 26; Timothy H. O'Sullivan/Civil War Photographs, 1861–1865/Library of Congress, 32; Samuel A. Cooley/Civil War Photographs, 1861–1865/Library of Congress, 35; MPI/Archive Photos/Getty Images, 36–37; Mathew B. Brady/Civil War Photographs, 1861–1865/Library of Congress, 40–41; Taylor & Huntington/Civil War Photograph Collection/Library of Congress, 43

Library of Congress Cataloging-in-Publication Data
Library of Congress Cataloging-in-Publication Data is available on the Library of Congress website.

ISBN
978-1-64493-084-7 (hardcover)
978-1-64493-163-9 (paperback)
978-1-64493-321-3 (ebook pdf)
978-1-64493-242-1 (hosted ebook)

Printed in the United States of America
Mankato, MN
012020

ABOUT THE AUTHOR

Tom Streissguth has written more than 100 works of nonfiction, including works of history, biography, geography, and current events. He has also built a popular website, The Archive of American Journalism, that collects interesting stories from historic and important newspapers.

TABLE OF CONTENTS

CHAPTER 1

SHERMAN'S DILEMMA

In September 1864, General William Tecumseh Sherman captured Atlanta, Georgia. His soldiers camped in the city's smoking ruins. The Union's artillery had done massive damage. Huge fires had burned homes and buildings to the ground. Atlanta's factories had produced weapons and supplies for the Confederate army. And the city was located along a major shipping route. Both facts made it a key target for the Union army.

William Tecumseh Sherman was one of the Union army's most famous generals.

Sherman's troops had begun marching toward Atlanta in the spring. They had fought several battles along the way. Now, the Confederate defenders had abandoned the city. Most of the **civilians** had fled. Sherman ordered those who remained to leave.

Then, he planned his next move. He could turn back north to attack the main Confederate army in Tennessee. Or, he could continue east toward the Atlantic Ocean. Staying in Atlanta was not an option. The city didn't have enough food for Sherman's soldiers, and supply posed a problem. The Union army used trains to send food, weapons, and equipment. To reach Atlanta, these trains had to travel hundreds of miles through Confederate territory. Guards had to stand along the way to protect the trains. An attack could keep supplies from reaching the Union soldiers.

Sherman's armies set up camp inside the city of Atlanta, Georgia.

If Sherman ordered his troops forward, he would have to extend these supply lines even more. Longer lines would be even easier to attack. Sherman's soldiers could end up without food or **reinforcements**.

Sherman sent 60,000 soldiers back to fight the Confederate army in Tennessee. The remaining 62,000 soldiers would march east. To keep them supplied, Sherman created a bold new plan.

CHAPTER 2

A NEW KIND OF WAR

The US Civil War began in April 1861. Over the next three years, many bloody battles raged. Thousands of soldiers and civilians died. But neither the Union nor the Confederacy gained much ground. By the summer of 1864, the armies had reached a stalemate. In some battles, soldiers dug trenches and struggled to get past the other side's defenses. Both sides prepared for a long and hard winter of fighting.

Many Civil War battles took place in Virginia.

General Sherman wanted to bring the fighting to a swift end. He planned to send his troops east from Atlanta. The soldiers would travel all the way to Savannah, Georgia. Then they would take control of the city's port on the Atlantic Ocean. The journey would cover 285 miles (459 km). It would also introduce a new kind of war.

Up to this point, most Civil War generals had focused on fighting enemy armies. Generals on both sides had gone to military schools such as the US Military Academy at West Point. They studied famous battles of the past. They learned the **tactics** armies used to win.

Sherman had attended West Point. But he believed ending the war would take more than winning battles. Instead, he planned to damage the South's **morale**. He hoped its leaders would surrender if people thought they couldn't win.

⚑ By damaging buildings and supplies, Sherman made it difficult for the Confederate army to fight.

To meet this goal, Sherman planned a scorched-earth **campaign**. In this strategy, an army destroys the land around it. The soldiers take the area's crops and livestock. They also damage buildings. That way, the opposing army cannot use them. The soldiers also take apart roads and railroads. This prevents the opposing army from sending supplies.

Sherman's soldiers would march across northern Georgia. Farmers in this region grew vegetables, cotton, and other crops. They brought their goods to Savannah and other ports to ship them all over the world.

During the march, Sherman's armies would not use supply lines. Instead, they would take whatever they needed from the land around them. Sherman hoped the invasion would make

Southerners feel powerless against the Union army. If Southerners believed their side had no hope of winning, they might pressure their leaders to make a **truce**.

Sherman submitted his plan to General Ulysses S. Grant, the overall commander of the Union forces. Grant was not happy that Sherman planned to go against traditional military strategy. Grant thought the Union should focus on defeating the Confederate armies. But Sherman was a successful general. He had won several key battles and captured Atlanta. Grant gave him permission to move ahead.

THINK ABOUT IT ◁

If you were General Grant, would you have approved Sherman's plan? Why or why not?

CHAPTER 3

THE MARCH BEGINS

Sherman's 62,000 soldiers left Atlanta on November 15, 1864. Right away, Sherman cut his supply lines. His troops would no longer get supplies from the North. Instead, they gathered food and other goods from the land around them. They also destroyed railroads, towns, and farms.

Judson Kilpatrick led the **cavalry**. The rest of the soldiers formed two long columns. Henry Slocum led the Army of Georgia on the left.

Sherman (seated, center) worked with a team of generals during his march to the sea.

Oliver Howard commanded the Army of the Tennessee on the right.

The two columns marched approximately 30 miles (48 km) apart. Sherman planned each column's route carefully. He set out their targets

ROUTES TO THE SEA

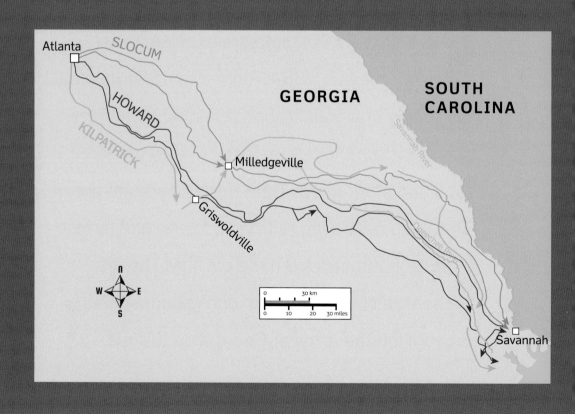

every night. Using the 1860 **census** and detailed maps, Sherman sent his troops through Georgia's richest farmland. The routes also passed through towns with factories. These places produced weapons and ammunition for the Confederate armies. Without them, the Confederates would run low on supplies.

Sherman planned to disrupt the supply of food, too. Union troops took crops and livestock from the region's farms. The soldiers had orders to destroy homes only if people resisted. But sometimes they destroyed other property, too.

Meanwhile, the main Confederate army was back in Tennessee. Instead of defending Georgia, the Confederate generals ordered attacks on the Union supply lines. They hoped to lure Sherman back to Tennessee. There, they planned to defeat him in a traditional battle. But their plan failed.

Sherman continued east. For most of the march, his armies faced almost no resistance. Only small local **militias** fought back. These units recruited boys and older men from local towns and farms. Many were poorly equipped and barely trained.

Confederate cavalry killed, wounded, or captured a few Union stragglers. But these Southern troops were no match for the massive Union armies. In fact, the only major battle took place near Griswoldville.

The Union cavalry, led by Kilpatrick, invaded this small town on November 21. They captured trains carrying military supplies. They also burned factories. The Confederate cavalry, led by Joseph Wheeler, fought Union troops patrolling the fields outside the town. Men on horseback skirmished along the trails, firing rifles and sending up shouts.

▲ Joseph Wheeler's cavalry followed Sherman's soldiers as they marched toward the Atlantic Ocean.

On November 22, Confederate militiamen joined the fight. The soldiers formed lines and advanced on the Union troops. Union soldiers from Howard's column set their lines at the edge of a field, using logs and rails to form a barricade.

In contrast, the Confederates had no cover. They suffered heavy losses as they crossed the field. The Battle of Griswoldville ended quickly. The Confederates retreated, and Sherman's armies continued marching east.

DOLLY SUMNER LUNT

Sherman's march began during the fall harvest. As the soldiers swept through Georgia, they left very little food behind. For example, Dolly Sumner Lunt owned a large plantation near Covington, Georgia. Union troops arrived at her home on November 19. Lunt asked them for protection, but they raided her house instead.

Lunt described the events in her diary: "To my smokehouse, my dairy, pantry, kitchen and cellar, like famished wolves they come, breaking locks and whatever is in their way."[1] The soldiers took the food Lunt had been storing. "The thousand pounds of meat in my smokehouse is gone in a twinkling, my flour, my meat, my lard, butter, eggs, pickles of various kinds—both in vinegar and brine—wine, jars and jugs are all gone."[2]

The Union soldiers also killed her livestock. "My eighteen fat turkeys, my hens, chickens, and

 Many plantations in Georgia grew cotton.

fowls, my young pigs are shot down in my yard and hunted as if they were rebels themselves."[3]

Lunt and her household depended on these food sources to survive the winter. Without these stores, they would likely starve. Lunt tried asking one soldier to stop the raid. But it was no use. He told her that he was just following orders.

1. Dolly Sumner Lunt. *A Woman's Wartime Journal*. New York: The Century Co., 1918. 22.
2. Lunt. *Wartime Journal*. 22–23.
3. Lunt. *Wartime Journal*. 23.

CHAPTER 4

ON TO MILLEDGEVILLE

As his soldiers continued marching toward the Atlantic Ocean, Sherman worked to keep their **objectives** secret. He didn't want the Confederates to learn where or how he planned to attack. So, Sherman had his armies cut telegraph lines as they traveled through Georgia. The soldiers would have no communication with the North. That way, the Confederates could not send or intercept any messages.

Sherman's soldiers tear up a railroad track.

Instead, Confederate leaders had to guess Sherman's plans. There were several important cities along the way that would make good targets for a Union attack. Augusta lay north of the route. Macon lay to the south. Both cities had factories, shops, and railroad stations.

But Sherman ordered General Slocum to march the left column toward Milledgeville. At the time, this town served as the capital of Georgia. It lay directly on the path between Atlanta and Savannah.

On November 23, some of Slocum's troops reached the city's outskirts. The Union soldiers found no defenders. The main Confederate armies were still off fighting in Tennessee and Virginia.

Desperate, Georgia's governor called civilians to form militias. All men between the ages of 16 and 65 were asked to join. Prisoners in local jails

were offered freedom if they agreed to fight. But the small Southern forces lacked weapons and training. They could not stop the massive Union armies. And some places, such as Milledgeville, were left undefended. Slocum's soldiers took over in just a few hours.

Slocum's troops celebrated Thanksgiving in Milledgeville by burning the city's factories and destroying its railroad station. They also looted the capitol building. The Union soldiers destroyed books and other documents they found inside it.

Bummers gathered food and supplies from local farms and towns.

They even held a mock session of the Georgia legislature. They voted unanimously for the state to leave the Confederacy and rejoin the Union.

Meanwhile, Sherman took over the governor's mansion and set up a headquarters. There, he prepared to continue on toward the Atlantic Ocean. Slocum's troops left Milledgeville on November 24. And Howard's troops kept marching east from Griswoldville.

The soldiers marched up to 15 miles (24 km) each day. Groups called pioneers traveled ahead of the main columns. The pioneers served as scouts. They found a path for the rest of the soldiers to follow. Pioneers cleared and repaired the roads and made sure bridges were safe to cross. They also looked for Confederate troops or militias that might attack.

Groups of bummers followed the pioneers. Their job was to gather food. Bummers collected crops and livestock from fields and farmhouses. They used horses, mules, and wagons to bring these supplies back to the main columns.

THINK ABOUT IT ◀

In what ways would a militia be more helpful than a traditional army? In what ways would it be less helpful?

CHARLES KERR

During the march, thousands of black people escaped slavery to join the Union army. They often worked as pioneers. But some Union leaders treated them cruelly. One example was Brigadier General Jefferson C. Davis.

In December 1864, his unit neared Ebenezer Creek. Davis had his men make a temporary pontoon bridge across the ice-cold water. He told the escaped slaves with his unit to stay behind. Confederate cavalry were nearby, Davis explained, and there might be fighting ahead.

When the last Union soldier crossed the creek, Davis had the bridge taken out of the water. The escaped slaves were stranded on the other side. And the Confederate soldiers were closing in.

A Union soldier named Charles Kerr described what happened next. He wrote that the stranded black people "raised their hands and implored

▲ Scandal followed Union general Jefferson C. Davis after his brutal actions at Ebenezer Creek.

from the corps commander the protection they had been promised."[1]

But Davis would not put the bridge back. So, people tried to cross the rushing water on their own. "With cries of anguish and despair," Kerr wrote, "men, women and children rushed by hundreds into the turbid stream."[2] Many of them drowned. Confederate soldiers killed others who stayed behind.

1. James Lee McDonough. *William Tecumseh Sherman.* New York: Norton, 2016. 526.
2. McDonough. *William Tecumseh Sherman.* 526.

CHAPTER 5

TAKING SAVANNAH

As the Union troops neared the Atlantic Ocean, their journey became more difficult. The land in this area was swampy. The soldiers' supplies also began to run low. They needed to link up with Union supply ships in Savannah's port. To do this, the two columns would take slightly different routes. Slocum's troops would march toward the Savannah River. Howard's column would follow the Ogeechee River instead.

Built along the Ogeechee River, Fort McAllister protected the city of Savannah, Georgia.

Cavalry commander Judson Kilpatrick was known for making daring and intense attacks.

Meanwhile, Kilpatrick's cavalry rode toward Camp Lawton. This Confederate prison camp held more than 10,000 Union soldiers. Kilpatrick had orders to take the camp and set them free. But its commanders had guessed that Sherman would try to do this. They fled as the Union troops approached. They moved the prisoners, too. So, Kilpatrick came back to join the main columns.

By December 10, both columns had reached the outskirts of Savannah. A Union fleet waited just off the coast. These ships carried food and supplies. The Ogeechee River would provide an easy route to reach the ships. The river wound down south of Savannah to the ocean. But to get down the river, the Union army would have to capture Fort McAllister. This Confederate fort stood just south of Savannah and defended the city's port.

The fort was a key Confederate stronghold. But only a small force, led by Major George Anderson, defended it. Anderson had placed land mines all around the fort. These small underground bombs would explode if soldiers stepped on them.

Obstacles known as abatis also surrounded the fort. These obstacles were made from bundles of tree trunks with sharpened points. Confederate soldiers set them up to slow attackers.

Union troops would have to approach the fort with caution. Sherman sent Kilpatrick's cavalry ahead to scout the area. Several cannons lined the fort's tall earthen walls. Soldiers inside the fort could use openings called embrasures to fire down on attackers. But the scouts saw only a few hundred defenders inside. Sherman decided to attack.

A division of Union troops approached the fort on December 13. General William Hazen ordered the men to spread out. He hoped to prevent heavy losses from cannon fire and mines.

At a signal, the Union troops charged ahead. They forced their way through the abatis and

After capturing Fort McAllister, Sherman's soldiers carried away wheelbarrows filled with ammunition.

attacked the Confederate defenders inside the fort. Anderson's outnumbered men fought back. But the battle was over in just a few minutes.

The Union now controlled Savannah's port. Sherman had a secure supply line to the North. On December 22, he telegraphed President Abraham Lincoln, offering the city of Savannah as a Christmas gift. Lincoln thanked Sherman, encouraging him to proceed as he saw fit.

CHAPTER 6

TURNING NORTH

Sherman's army spent Christmas and New Year's in Savannah. But the campaign was not over. Sherman was preparing for another march. This time, he planned to head north into South Carolina. This state had been the first to **secede** from the Union. Sherman wanted to make an example of it. He told his soldiers to cause damage like they had done in Georgia. He hoped the harsh attacks would help end the war sooner.

Sherman's troops caused even worse destruction in South Carolina than they had in Georgia.

On February 1, 1865, Sherman's armies left Savannah. Their route included several cities. But Columbia, the state's capital, was their main objective. Only a few Confederate troops

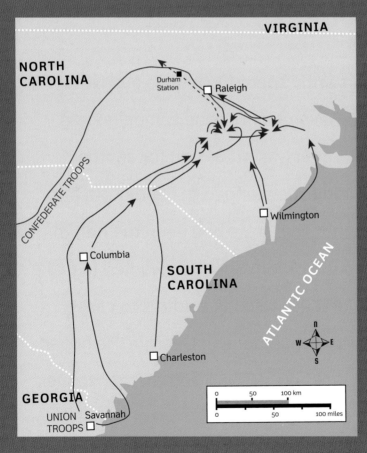

THE CAROLINAS CAMPAIGN

VIRGINIA

NORTH CAROLINA

Durham Station

Raleigh

CONFEDERATE TROOPS

Wilmington

Columbia

SOUTH CAROLINA

ATLANTIC OCEAN

Charleston

GEORGIA

UNION TROOPS   Savannah

N
W   E
S

0   50   100 km
0   50   100 miles

defended this city. Faced with Sherman's massive armies, they retreated. On February 17, the Union soldiers marched into Columbia unopposed.

Sherman continued into North Carolina. By April, he was ready to march into Virginia and help General Grant fight the army of Robert E. Lee. But Grant's troops had finally broken through the Confederate lines. They took the capital city of Richmond, Virginia. Lee surrendered on April 9.

General Joseph Johnston had been leading the Confederate efforts against Sherman's march. But after Lee's defeat, Johnston was ready to surrender as well.

On April 26, Sherman and Johnston met in a farmhouse near Durham, North Carolina. There, Johnston and the Confederates agreed to stop all fighting against the Union. The Confederacy's two main armies had laid down their weapons.

CHAPTER 7

AN IMPORTANT SHIFT

Sherman's march to the sea played a key role in the Union victory. From the start, his main goal was ending the war as soon as possible. The longer the fighting continued, the more people on both sides would be hurt or killed. By convincing the South to give up, Sherman believed he could help save lives.

Historians agree that Sherman's march helped end the war. It was devastating for the South.

Sherman's soldiers march in a victory parade in Washington, DC, in May 1865.

The Union armies left a path of destruction through northern Georgia. Soldiers burned hundreds of houses, fields, and barns. They also tore up miles of railroad tracks. Soldiers heated the rails in massive fires. Then they wrapped the hot rails around large tree trunks. The rails hardened as they cooled, making the tracks impossible to repair. The twisted rails became known as Sherman's neckties.

The Union troops also took massive amounts of food and livestock. They seized nearly 5,000 horses and 13,000 cattle. And Georgia farmers lost 9.5 million pounds (4.3 million kg) of corn.

These losses hurt the Confederate armies. Confederate troops could not get the food or supplies they needed. But civilians also struggled to survive. Without railroads, farmers couldn't transport their goods. And cut telegraph wires

▲ Soldiers burned wooden railroad ties beneath the rails.

made it impossible to send messages. Many people left their homes and fields. In some places, the economy took years to recover.

Sherman believed a severe approach was necessary to get the desired effect on the South's morale. But critics claimed he violated the rules of war. They opposed the march's focus on civilians.

Sherman's strategy continues to be studied, imitated, and debated today.

Because farmers and their families weren't soldiers, the critics reasoned, armies should not try to harm them or their property.

The march affected black Southerners, too. As Sherman's armies passed through the South, enslaved people sometimes escaped to follow them. Sherman supported setting slaves free. But he didn't want them following his troops. He worried they would slow his movement. Some of his commanders, such as Davis, shared this view. Racism was also common among Union soldiers. The former slaves often faced discrimination.

Sherman's march remains controversial. But its impact is undeniable. His tactics changed the course of modern warfare. Other military leaders would follow his example. They damaged food or supplies that could be used by opposing troops. This policy of attacking entire areas of land, not just enemy armies, became known as total war.

THINK ABOUT IT ◁

Can you think of other armies that directed attacks toward civilians? What goals do you think their leaders hoped to achieve?

FOCUS ON
SHERMAN'S MARCH TO THE SEA

Write your answers on a separate piece of paper.

1. Write a paragraph summarizing the main ideas of Chapter 2.

2. Sherman wanted to bring a faster end to the war. Do you think that reason justifies the damage his march caused? Why or why not?

3. Which city did Sherman attack on the way to Savannah?

    A. Augusta

    B. Macon

    C. Milledgeville

4. Why did Sherman's troops destroy railroad tracks along their march?

    A. to prevent civilians from escaping

    B. to collect iron for Union factories

    C. to stop Confederates from sending supplies

Answer key on page 48.

GLOSSARY

campaign
A series of military activities, often in a certain area or using a certain kind of fighting, planned to achieve a goal.

cavalry
A military force with troops who serve on horseback.

census
A count of an area's population.

civilians
People who are not in the military.

militias
Groups of citizens trained to carry out military actions, usually during times of emergency.

morale
The mood of a group of people, especially people in a difficult situation.

objectives
The goals or targets of a military campaign.

reinforcements
Additional supplies of soldiers.

secede
To formally withdraw from a political group or nation.

tactics
Planned actions that are used to achieve a certain goal.

truce
An agreement to stop fighting for a period of time.

TO LEARN MORE

BOOKS

Cummings, Judy Dodge. *Civil War Leaders*. Minneapolis: Abdo Publishing, 2017.

Grayson, Robert. *The U.S. Civil War: Why They Fought*. North Mankato, MN: Capstone, 2016.

MacCarald, Clara. *Children During the Civil War*. Lake Elmo, MN: Focus Readers, 2019.

NOTE TO EDUCATORS

Visit **www.focusreaders.com** to find lesson plans, activities, links, and other resources related to this title.

INDEX

Answer Key: 1. Answers will vary; **2.** Answers will vary; **3.** C; **4.** C